Life in a Bubble

A Testimony Never Told

LAKENDRA L. BODY

LIFE IN A BUBBLE

Published by Lee's Press and Publishing Company
www.LeesPress.net

This document is published by Lee's Press and Publishing Company located in the United States of America. It is protected by the United States Copyright Act, all applicable state laws and international copyright laws. The information in this document is accurate to the best of the ability of Lakendra L. Body at the time of writing. The content of this document is subject to change without notice.

ISBN-13: *Paperback*
9798451463833

Table of Contents

Acknowledgements 5

Dedication... 10

Introduction 11

What is Depression? 13

What is Anxiety? 14

What is Grief? 16

What's Happening to Me? 17

Devastated 20

Losing Hope.. 25

Pressing On 29

Controlling Anxiety 33

Slowly Progressing 35

A Major Progress...................................... 37

The Set Back... 40

GOD Burst the Bubble................................ 42

Pre-Prepared... 46

Understanding Death................................. 50

A Major Decline 52

I Died Mentally, He Died Spiritually 57

Life Without Him...................................... 66

The Church Termination Letter 69

The Greatness of GOD 73

Healed! Delivered and Set Free 74

Acknowledgements

To GOD - First, I want to take the time to thank you for life today. I want to thank you for looking over me when I could not find the words to pray to you. I thank you for never leaving me, nor forsaking me. I thank you for your grace and mercy that brought me through. Every morning, I wake up, I continue this journey because of you. Every time, when I felt I wanted to give up, you were always there with another option to change my mind. When I drifted off and had negative thoughts, you gave me a sign. I cannot thank you enough for bursting that bubble. I love you and I'll never give up on you because not once did you give up on me.

To My Mom - Thank you for sticking by me and never giving up on me. I appreciate your love and patience through my condition and with your encouraging words, I knew I would bounce back. I'll never forget the times you checked on me to make sure I was ok. I can still remember like it was yesterday, when you would get up with me all times of nights and comfort me when I could not sleep. That was a mother's love. To make a long appreciation short, I just want to thank you for being right there for me like a mother should.

To My Grandmother - I know I gave you a major scare but I'm sorry, I did not feel it coming myself. I applaud you for being by my side and taking out the time to say a special prayer for me every day. I thank you for making calls every day to make sure people prayed for me. I can't thank you enough for helping me keep the faith and know that GOD would heal me.

To my late great grandfather – I am so glad that GOD allowed you to be there with me during my condition. When I saw you get on your knees every night, I knew that someday I would be healed and set free. While going through this darkness, I thought back to the times you would take me to church on Sunday's as a little girl, which lead me to the scripture that reads, "train up a child the way they should go and they will not depart from it" Proverbs 22:6 (KJV). I realized that you had trained me up and now I have to take actions for myself. When I realized what I needed to do, I got on my knees every night and prayed to GOD just like you, because I knew I wanted to be healed! Continue to rest peacefully Dad!

To My aunt's Toya, Annette, Jackie, Debra, Rosie, and Brenda - I appreciate everything you did to help me during my time of need. I know it was difficult trying to understand my condition, when I barely could explain how I felt myself. I thank you for reaching out to various Nurses and Counselors to help me through this process. Most of all, I thank you for caring and never giving up on me.

To Elder Jose Watson - I appreciate you and your wife for taking out the time to use your anointed hands to lay on me. I truly thank GOD for calling Pastors and Missionaries like you to help and see people through like myself. I heard you preach, sing, and lay hands on people before, but I did not grasp the concept until I was the one you had to lay hands on. That Sunday, at the altar you claimed that I was healed and set free and I was! I just had to wait on the Lord.

To the late Missionary Geneva Smith - I still have visions of you grabbing that oil to pray and lay hands on me. I can hear you asking me to repeat after you as you sang, "I'm free." It was what I needed to be free from everything that had a burden on me. I appreciate you for doing that for me. I love you! Continue to rest peacefully.

To Nurse Barbra Williams - When I first started to have symptoms, you knew it was serious and that I needed immediate medical attention. Thank you for leading me to the right doctors, looking out for me when I came back to school, praying with me, for me, and encouraging me that I would get better.

To Mrs. Charlotte Thurman - From you sacrificing your lunch break to bring me lunch, giving me a comfortable environment to eat lunch were all acts of a caring counselor. I'm sorry that life ended up the way it did for you. You were there for me no matter the circumstance. One of the reasons I stop by your room when I visit the Nursing Home is to remind you of how much I love and appreciate you for everything that you did to help me.

To Mrs. Donna Rush - I can remember being the sharpest student in your Mississippi Studies Class. I knew things that many of the other students didn't, like the president of Mississippi Valley State University and the tax assessor of Belzoni. As I started to miss days, I knew if I was missed by a teacher it would be you. I thank you for being a caring teacher and understanding my condition at the time.

To Mrs. Mary Toy Reed - Thank you for taking the time to sit down and evaluate what was really wrong with me. As I explained to you how I was feeling, tears began to roll down your face and I knew then that you felt the pain I was going through. I appreciate your prayers, concerns, and encouraging words. It really helped me through the journey. You were such a loving teacher.

To my best friend, my coworker, Audriel Carpenter - I know you got tired of me telling you every day that I would write a book, I know you were wondering when. Well, here it goes!! My very first book. Thank you for believing in me, taking out the time to read my draft over and over again. I really appreciate you for being such a great and loyal friend.

Last but not least, to my publisher William Lee - Thanks for believing in me and helping to make my dream come true. You're the best!

Dedication

I dedicate this book to everyone who is battling anxiety, depression, and/or grief. I want everyone who may encounter it in the future, to be encouraged. Don't Give up. Don't give in. Give it to God. He will work it out right on time!

In Remembrance of

Hugh "Junior" Body ……………..1939-2017

Kathy Grace Smith …………….1994-2014

Aloysius Mabry ………………..1986-2019

Introduction

Sweaty palms, racing heart, a weird feeling, paranoid mind, a shaky body, a scared soul, and afraid that I would die and wake up in a funeral home cold. Truth be told I was that girl drowning in this thing called depression. There was no way, I was going to fold. The enemy's plan was to take me out, but GOD had my back and I'm grateful for that. If I had a million tongues, I still could not thank Him enough for bringing me out. I have enemies til this day that have done me wrong, but I still would not wish this condition on anyone. While going through this, I only wanted to get better and be myself again so I tried GOD like never before. My faith in God was so strong, I believed that I could be back to my normal self in the next 5 minutes. I tried doctors, and medication and I still was not getting well. I always heard my Grandfather say, "If that man up above cannot fix it, then nobody else can" so I knew if I wanted to be healed, I had to talk to GOD. Not just one day, one night, but every single night. I am currently 21-years-old, and a resident of Belzoni, MS. I am the oldest of three children, a certified nursing assistant (CAN) and I recently received my Associate's Degree of Arts in Pre-Allied Health on May 10, 2019. I suffered from depression, grief, and anxiety at a young age. I was that STRONG friend, daughter, sister, granddaughter, cousin, and student that needed to be checked on. I was in a bubble that needed to be burst. The bubble could not be burst by anyone but a man named GOD! Once you're done reading my book you will understand the meaning of depression, anxiety, and grief. Understanding how serious it is, what those things will do to you, and how GOD HEALED ME from it all.

What is Depression?

Depression is defined by a mood disorder that causes a persistent feeling of sadness and loss of interest. It affects how you feel, think, and behave and it can lead to a variety of emotional and physical moments. Every day I researched depression and ways I could get better. It had me feeling weird. In my mind, I always thought that I was dying. I would cry 5 to 6 times a day. The things that would interest me before, did not interest me anymore. I would yell for help in moments of panicking. During my research, I learned that there are a variety of factors that cause depression: biological differences, brain chemistry, hormones, and also inherited traits. I came to the conclusion that it was an inherited trait from my parents and family. When I was twelve-years-old, my mom was diagnosed with depression and became unable to care for my siblings and I. Therefore, my grandmother took up the slack. I watched her sit on the couch and cry for days. One night, I witnessed her attempting to take pills, trying to commit suicide because depression took over that bad. My mom seeked for help and was placed on medication that never took. Later in life, I discovered that my paternal grandmother also suffered from depression and grief. As a result, she had been placed in several different facilities for healing. Depression decided to come after me, out of all my father's children, but it could not get the victory after all the nights of dropping down on my knees praying to the good Lord.

What is Anxiety?

Anxiety is an intense, excessive, persistent worry and fear about everyday situations. Fast heart rate, rapid breathing, sweating, and feeling tired may occur. This definition also showed, its ugly symptoms as well. Anxiety presents itself in many different ways. It has the desire to control people and events. It causes you to have difficulty getting to sleep. Often times, it will have you feeling agitated or angry. It will have you avoiding activities or events, and even struggling to pay attention and focus. When you just can't seem to control the disorder, it will have you feeling worried about things a lot. When anxiety attacks came upon me, my heart rate increased, my breathing was intense and I would sweat and feel tired all the time. I always feared that something would happen to me at any given moment. There were moments where I felt like I was losing my mind. As I researched depression even more, I also researched anxiety. I compared the symptoms of anxiety and depression and they had almost the same symptoms. There was a slight difference. While researching this information, I thought day after day that there was no hope for me. I questioned my family and people around me about it these symptoms but no one had ever experienced it before. It seems to me, that it all appeared out of nowhere. I had no clue what caused this. In my mind, I didn't care what I needed to do, to get well. I just wanted to be healed and set free. At that moment, I felt like I was alone because I was the only one going through it at the time. While searching online, I read about other people's terrifying experiences but they were all out of state. I knew there had to be at least one person in Mississippi that encountered this problem, but evidently, they kept it a secret and not wanting anyone to know. This was compared to having cancer, sickle cell, diabetes and there was no way I was the first one to experience it.

What is Grief?

Grief is a multifaceted response to loss, particularly to the loss of someone or something that died, to which a bond or affection was formed. There are five stages: denial, anger, bargaining, depression, and acceptance. Every stage was rough for me during the time I lost my church member but the acceptance stage was a major one. I could not accept the fact that the person was gone. After hearing all the news of the persons death and seeing an obituary, I could not accept it. That person was Justin, the first young person that I had bonded with. Following the death of my great-grandfather Robert Bullock, my great-grandmother Ethel Bullock, my cousin Kathy Grace Smith, my uncle Tahiti Banks, my grandfather Hugh Junior Body, my aunt Tonja Thomas, and last but not least, my best friend Aloysius Mabry. There were some people I fail to mention because our bond wasn't as strong as the seven mentioned above. I grieved over them all, but most of them got easier with the exception of two. I still have moments of grief, over my great-grandfather and cousin. Death has never been easy for me, regardless if the person was related to me or not. The bible says, "To be absent from the body, is to be present with the Lord." I pray that one day, GOD will help me understand exactly what he meant without me wondering or grieving after the fact. I have gotten better through the years and I thank GOD for never leaving my side, healing my broken heart, and easing my grief.

What's Happening To Me?

It was right after Thanksgiving break, the year of 2012. I went back to school at HCHS on a Monday, like a normal day. I ate breakfast and went to the gym before classes started. That was everybody's morning routine. While sitting in the gym, I began to lose oxygen, I got hot, I could not swallow, and everything around me was blurry. I felt that something was happening to me. I asked a classmate if I could use her phone to call my mom, but I just couldn't seem to dial the number. I quickly gave her phone back, ran to the gym lobby to tell my cousin Equana Jones that I was not feeling well. Equana was a teacher at HCHS. She insisted that I get checked by the nurse, so I quickly went to Nurse Williams office. I explained to her, what was going on and she told me that I should be seen by a doctor. Nurse Williams called my mom to pick me up. At the time, my mom didn't have a car, so she borrowed my uncle's suburban to pick me up. When we got in the vehicle, she began to question me. "Is there someone bullying you?" "Is someone trying to fight you?" I replied, "NO" with tears in my eyes. At that moment, I was still having the symptoms from earlier in the gym, but I didn't know what was actually wrong. While traveling to my grandfather's house from the school, I began to panic and lose oxygen again. I told my mom that I couldn't breathe. She let the window down so I could get air but that was not working at all. While the truck was still moving, I jumped out and ran to the first house I could see, Ms. Sista Hooker's house. I couldn't speak at the time, so I grabbed the first cup I could find and got water out of her sink. By the time I got the water down, my mom ran in to check on me and explained to Ms. Hooker what was going on with me. While my mom tried calming me down, Ms. Hooker dialed 911. When the EMT arrived, they checked me and asked me what was going on. I told them I couldn't breathe. While checking my o2, the EMT lady explained that I was breathing just fine. They put me on the stretcher and drove me to the hospital. That was my first ambulance ride and I was so scared! The male EMT worker that rode in the back did a great job of calming me down. He began to make conversation with me. He asked, "was I afraid of dying?" I told him, "yes I was afraid to die." He then began telling me a story about how a man died on the stretcher in front of him, he said he hit the man in the chest and he came back alive. I was listening well, until I saw my grandfather's blue ford truck from the window of the ambulance. My late great-grandfather, Huge Junior Body was my hero and my backbone. I could tell him things I could not tell anyone else. At that moment, I felt I really needed him, he was the only person that could pray for me and I knew I would be well in no time. We arrived at the hospital and my grandfather was right behind the ambulance waiting for me. When they checked me in, the doctor told me that my throat was closing up. When she told me that, I began to panic again and question if she was sure that was the problem! I questioned her because she was really old and it seemed as if she had a vision problem because of the way she squinted her eyes to examine my throat. When she assured me that was the problem, my grandfather looked at me and told me that I would be just fine. My Dad showed up but at the time, we did not have a father and daughter bond. I had all types of thoughts running through my mind. My mind wandered off into deep thoughts about how I would live if my throat continued to close up, I had eaten or drank something that had caused my throat to close. My mind was blank, I could not even remember what I had eaten in the cafeteria that morning. That's how terrified and shaken up I was at the moment. When she told me, what was going on with me, it seemed like everything in my body had shut down. I had never been so scared before in my life, until I heard that. I am grateful that I did not have a heart attack. While crying out to my mom, I asked her, "what's happening to me?" I could see the hurt in her eyes. While looking in her eyes I could see that she wished she had an answer, but all she knew was what the doctors told us. I had this feeling over me as if something could happen to me at any moment. As I tried fighting it, the feeling fought back even harder. I had never in my life felt such a feeling. These feelings had me stuck in one spot, not wanting to move. I had to force myself to move, every step I made, I got tired. I felt as if I had carried a ton of bricks.

Devastated!

The doctor at Humphreys County Memorial Hospital referred me to an Ear, Nose, and Throat specialist in Greenwood, MS. Again, my mom did not have a car at the time, so she asked her friend to drive us there while my grandfather went back to work. With my throat closing up, I was thinking the ambulance should have taken me. I thought wrong! That was the longest ride ever to Greenwood, knowing that my throat was closing up. I laid out on the back seat in one position all the way there. When we arrived at the clinic, the doctor examined my throat and he said that everything looked just fine. I could not believe the words he was saying, because I knew it was something going on with me. The next day my mom decided to take me to Gorton Clinic and the nurse practitioner Emily Aust told me that I was experiencing anxiety and a major nerve problem. The day after that, I felt like everything was closing in on me. From walls, to trees, doors, car windows, etc. My mom decided to take me to Indianola Family Medical Center. I explained my symptoms to Mrs. Terri Rowland, NP at the facility. As I was explaining, with tears in my eyes about the symptoms, she too became teary eyed too. She said to me, "sweetie you are dealing with anxiety mixed with grief and depression," I instantly cried harder. I began to think, what could I possibly be depressed about at 16-years-old in the 9th grade! How did I develop anxiety? She prescribed five different types of medications and told me to try them out and see how they would work. I went on day by day, taking the medicine and each day I was declining. I felt spaced out! I could not eat nor sleep. I cried every single day. I did not want to go outside. No one understood how I felt and I could not tell them. It was a feeling that was hard to explain. At times, it felt like my soul was leaving my body. I began to get terrified of sleeping alone and being in places by myself. I started sleeping with my mom and begging her to keep the light on. Weeks passed by and I still did not feel like myself. My body got weaker by the day. I didn't know if I would see the next day or not. I was breathing but it did not feel like I was at all. I was sleeping but I did not get any rest. When I was alert enough, I would ask someone if I had been to sleep or not. I missed months of school because I could not focus. My aunt Toya was an employee with Life Help at the time. She asked around about my situation and the workers recommended I seek help at an Institution in Jackson, MS Brentwood clinics. My mom made an appointment and I had to be there the next day. No one wanted me to go and stay alone but everyone wanted me to get well. My aunt Toya, drove us the next day. My mom had a bag packed for me because she knew I would have to stay. When we arrived there, they explained the rules to me about the things I could and couldn't have. The first thing I saw was, "NO CELL PHONES" but the plan was to sneak mines in anyway. While sitting in the waiting area, I saw one of my elementary classmates getting ready to be checked in as well. I felt a little better that I had seen someone I know, but not better enough to stay there without my phone. Soon they called me to the back, checked my vitals and my temperature was 101.3. They told me that they could not take me as a patient because I was ill. They gave my mom an option to take me to the ER for antibiotics and bring me back or take me home until I got well. I looked my mom in the eyes and said to her that I wanted to go home. That moment, I had faith the size of a mustard seed because I knew GOD could heal me without being placed in a facility. We traveled back to Belzoni, MS and I was back at square one with the same feelings. My family began to be there for me more and the only thing I wanted to do was lay around. The bed was taking my strength away and I got weaker by the day. I could barely stand on my own without shaking or having to take a seat. My aunt's Annette and Toya encouraged on a daily basis. I began to do exercises around the house to build my strength back up. When my strength started coming back, my mom forced me to go to school but by noon and she would have to pick me up because my anxiety was through the roof. During this time, a church member had been killed in a car accident. I had just broken up with my first love and he began to date my friend's sister, my uncle had ended up moving to Texas to avoid trouble. While everyone was sad about my church members' death, I was busy trying to encourage people and cheer them up. I felt some type of way about my first love dating my friend's sister but I did not care because I knew GOD had better waiting for me. With my uncle moving away, I thought about it as if he would have a better life and didn't have to deal with Belzoni and the drama anymore. I was thinking positive and on the bright side, not knowing that I would be experiencing anxiety, grief, and depression a couple of days later. The next weekend, it was time for my church members' funeral. His wake was held on a Friday at Smith Funeral Home. My aunt, uncle, and my mother decided to go view his body and I rode along with them. When we pulled up, it was time for us to go in but my mom made me stay in the car because she was afraid that I would have an anxiety attack. That really crushed my heart because I really wanted to show my respect to the family. We had just become the best of friends before he went to basic training and I just could not believe he was gone the moment he came back home to visit. The Pastor had just prayed for him months ago before leaving for training and the entire sanctuary wished him well. A week prior to that, I saw him at Double Quick getting something to eat. I just could not grasp the concept that he was gone. The next day they had his funeral. It was held at the High School auditorium. My mom did not allow me to attend the funeral either. I had to ask how things went and was only left with an obituary to read. That Sunday, I was forced to go to church knowing in my mind I would not see him standing at the door. Yes, he was an usher, he was handsome, quiet, and all of the mothers and deacons admired him for being such an intelligent young man and so did I. I had gone to funerals before his death and I had heard of people dying. It was family members who passed away before this occurred, but it did not hit me until I had to hear of someone dying at such a young age that I knew, oh so well. As time passed, I learned what grief really was, how bad it could make you feel, and that I had developed it along with what I was already facing. I began to ask GOD every night to help me through the process. Being that I had never experienced grief before, I cried a lot because I could not believe what was happening to me. I was scared. The devil had in my mind that I would never get well. He gave me thoughts that I would never be a normal kid again, nor further my education but GOD proved to him in the end that he was a lie. I was always told that you could never go wrong with the man up above on your side. Although, I did not feel my best, I still carried Him with me everywhere I went. Continuously, I asked Him for guidance and strength daily, from the time He woke me up those mornings until the time I went to sleep. The feeling brought me back to some lyrics of a song my uncle Homer often sang at church, "I can't even walk, without you holding my hand." The lyrics rang in my head day after day and sometimes I would sing it out loud because I knew it was nobody but GOD walking with me, holding my hand every step of the way.

Losing Hope

The month of December approached and I was still feeling the exact same way. No changes at all. As you read on, you will see that the process was very long. One third Sunday morning, while lying in the bed with my mom, Peter Popoff caught my attention on TV. I could see him anointing the people and they began to heal immediately. That took me back to when I was a little girl around the age of 5 and my mom and grandma took me to this church where my cousin Walter Goss Jr., "Tray" was preaching. He was praying for the people but at the same time, they were falling out as if they were dead. It scared me so bad that I vomited on the lady that fell beside me. My mom quickly rushed me to the bathroom and explained to me that it was ok and they were not dead. She told me they were being healed. She and I reminisced about that moment and she told me that I needed to be healed also just as the people did back at the church when I was age 5. We had service at my church that Sunday but instead we went to New Life St. Paul C.O.G.I.C., where I knew they would lay hands on me. At the time, the church was located on Fisk Street. As we walked in, they were still in Sunday school. My mom, aunt, grandma, and I proceeded to the back of the church as the late Missionary Geneva Smith and her daughter Pyron met with us and led us into the pastor's study. I explained to them what was going on with me. Missionary asked me had I ever heard of the song, "I

Am Free." I nodded yes and she asked me to sing it with her. While singing that song she and Pyron anointed me with oil and they prayed for me at that moment and wanted me to return back to regular service at 11:15. We returned back to service and as they began alter prayer, Elder Jose Watson called me up for a special prayer. I was always afraid of falling in the spirit but I did not care at that moment, I just wanted to be healed. I went up to the altar with a water bottle in my hand. I felt that I needed that water to survive. While Elder prayed for me, his wife Mrs. April Watson tried prying the water bottle out of my hand but at the time, I could not let it go. My eyes were open, my body was numb, I could hear him, but that was it. GOD was working on me. He prayed for me for at least 15 minutes. When he finished praying for me, I felt empty but I still felt a bit weird. Days passed and I just thought I should get on my knees and pray every night. I did that and I focused on this scripture; *"O Lord, if you heal me, I will be truly healed; if you save me, I will be truly saved."* **Jeremiah 17:14 NLT**

It had begun to be a cycle; I would look forward to getting on my knees to ask GOD to heal me each night. I would repeat this scripture until my mouth was tired. I just wanted to be normal again and I wanted to be healed. I wanted to be free from whatever it was that had me bound. By this time, word had spread to certain people that I was sick. I began to receive visitors from several pastors and family friends. Everyone was totally worried about me. I was worried about myself until I got down on my knees and began to know GOD for myself. See, I was always used to going to my Grandfather and close family members to solve all of my problems but in this situation, I had to do it on my own. I had to show GOD that I was trusting Him. I had to keep the faith and stay encouraged! I told GOD daily that if He didn't do anything else for me, I just wanted to be healed and normal again. I had gone to church as a child and I heard about GOD, but I didn't really understand who He was, until I went through this and tried Him for myself. I asked Him to forgive me for whatever I did to have this anxiety, grief, and depression. I asked Him to rebuke all demonic spirits that were trying to overtake me. I did not miss a night of getting on my knees, praying nor calling my grandmother to remind her to pray for me. I had no worries about my grandfather because I saw him get on his knees, faithfully, every night as a MAN to pray for his entire family. I would often hear him quote the bible scripture; *"Every knee shall bow, and every tongue must confess."* During my process, I finally understood what it actually meant. In other words, when praises go up, blessings come down. GOD saw me every night when I bowed to pray to Him, and being that it was a must from Him, He blessed me to be healed in spite of the mess the devil had me bound too. GOD knew that I would be healed in no time but I had to believe, in order for Him to deliver me. No, it did not happen the next day. No, it did not happen overnight. It took time, prayer, and most of all it took patience. The process humbled me more than I had ever been before. Basically, it was an eye opener for me to get my life right with GOD. See, before this happened to me, I didn't know GOD for myself at all, I had only heard of Him. Nowadays, I catch myself being glad that all of this happened to me because if it hadn't happened, I wouldn't know GOD for myself like I know Him now.

Pressing On

The month of January came and it was a new year, 2013. On New Year's Eve, I went to church at Christian Valley for watch night with my grandmother and aunt. Before I got depressed, I was a part of the praise team at my church and the members at Christian Valley requested us to do a praise dance. I did not want to participate because I had completely forgotten the dance. My mom told me that if I danced, I probably would feel better because that was something I loved to do. I did the dance that night but I still did not feel any better. I began to think about all the doctors I had gone to see and it had been 2 months and still not feeling like myself. I had one more clue in mind that could have been the problem. I thought, maybe someone had put a spell on me. Many people call it Voodoo; I asked my mom to take me to a witchcraft doctor. I had heard all of the stories about it before. Snakes coming out of people's mouths, people losing their minds, people eating random things, or walking around butt naked. Each time, I heard about witchcraft, I instantly got sad about the innocent people that did not get help in time so they ended up losing their lives from it. I truly though I was a victim until I had confirmation that I wasn't. As nosey as I was as a little girl, I never once heard anyone saying that a witchcraft Doctor stayed in Belzoni, MS. I knew her so well that she was just like an aunt to me. When I entered her house to get checked out, she told me that I was clean and she assured me if I was majorly witch crafted, that she would have known once I walked through her door. To be on the safe side, she checked me anyway. She started off by shuffling a deck of cards and asking me to make a wish. My wish was to be HEALED! While making a wish she began to sing a song I had never heard before. Then, she started to rub my legs down with Olive Oil. She told my mom that my nerves were in a wreck, I was depressed, and I had a lot balled up inside of me that I had not vented to anyone about. She prayed for me and told me to continue rubbing down with Olive Oil, drink warm milk at night, and continue to pray. Days after using the method she had given me; I began to feel a little bit at ease but at night when I drank the warm milk I felt as if I was floating on clouds. I was finally able to sleep and control myself and I started going back to school. I had fallen behind in school which was another burden that I had to bear. My peers and classmates questioned me daily about why I had not been to school. I lied to them, telling them I had Thyroid disease. Unfortunately, I was seriously diagnosed with an over active thyroid a year later. When I went back to school, everything felt brand new to me. I had heard of state testing approaching but I did not worry much because it was many months away. During that time, I tried to focus as much as I could and I tried to learn how to mingle again with my peers without them finding out. Daily, I tried to act normal like nothing was going on with me but deep down inside I was nervous, scared, and terrified that I would freak out. When I felt the anxiety coming on, I would ask the teacher if I could go to Nurse Williams office. Each time I went to her room she would pray for me, pray with me, read me a couple of bible scriptures and assure me that I would be just fine if I kept praying and depending on the Lord. I went to her office so much that my classmates began to ask why I always needed to go to the nurse. I never responded because it was not their business. I just wanted to be healed and set free without any negativity. At any minute, I always thought that I would have an anxiety attack. To prevent them, I kept gum in my pocket and water in my backpack at all times. The medication I was prescribed made me sick to my stomach, so I started to take it at night instead of in the morning. When I started taking the pills at night, the crying stopped, so that was a big plus for me. I no longer felt so emotional like I did before, so I did not have to worry about anyone coming up to me asking me what was wrong. My mingling got better and I began to be friends again with the people I was friends with before all of this happened to me. I got comfortable enough to tell the few friends I did have, about what was going on with me, but they still did not understand what I really meant. Years later, they remembered because a couple of them experienced the same thing after me. Without telling them my entire testimony, I told them the symptoms I was having, so they wouldn't feel alone like I did. Each time, someone came to me for help or advice with depression, grief, or anxiety, I made sure I was there for them and gave them my best advice. Not because I experienced it, but because GOD allowed me a chance to get out and be healed. I know if He did it for me, He could do the same for them.

Controlling Anxiety

I got the hang of going back to school and focusing on my work but I still had a few flaws. I did not eat in the cafeteria because of the noise and crowds. I did not attend assemblies in the gym nor the auditorium for the same exact reasons. The school counselor was Ms. Sophia Gray but at the time Mrs. Charlotte Thurman was filling in for her. Each day around lunchtime, Mrs. Thurman would come and get me out of my biology class to eat lunch in the office. We would have lunch together and she would talk to me about my situation, I would then go back to class and continue my work. After I was done eating, a couple of my classmates began to question me about the reason I did not go to the cafeteria or assemblies. I told them that crowds aggravated me but I did not go into details about my condition. My teachers knew about my condition but they did not share it with the students and I thanked them for that. After all of the rumors and lies, not one student knew what was really going on with me. Time passed and it was time for me to go back for a follow up at Indianola Family Medical Center. Mrs. Terri took me off all of my pills except one. To be honest I had flushed most of them down the toilet the day I was prayed for at church. I knew that GOD could heal me faster than any type of medication. From that moment, I had my mind set on trusting and believing Mrs, Terri had set me up to see this psychiatrist once a month in Jackson, MS. I started going but it discouraged me all over again. Every time I left out, I would cry a river and ask my mom not to take me back to that place again, I stopped paying attention to what the psychiatrist said and put my trust in GOD! Before I knew it, I was slowly getting back to myself. The depression was easing but I still had to deal with the anxiety attacks. It was tough but I discovered a method of how to control it with gum, candy, and prayer. Any time I felt an attack coming on I would put gum in my mouth followed by a small prayer; that always helped me through my day.

Slowly Progressing

As I continued to control my anxiety, I was progressing but it was a slow process. The time had come at school for state testing for Algebra 1 and Biology 1 I had no clue what I would do. GOD was in one ear telling me that it was already done and the devil was in the other ear telling me that I wouldn't be able to focus because of my situation. The teachers were serious about "subject area testing" because if the percentage of passing was not where it was, then it would fall back on them. The days got closer for the Algebra 1 test and I got terrified every time Mrs. Jamison opened her mouth and said something. The day of the test was rough for me. I had to deal with my anxiety plus test anxiety. I marked the best answer for every question but I still had doubt that I would pass. The results came back and surely, I did not pass. The test was required to graduate. Even though, I was only in the 9th grade, I still had time to pass before my senior year but I did not want to be classified as a freshman during my senior year. They gave everyone who failed a second chance to take the test. Every day, we had to stay after school for tutorial up until the day we had to retest. During my tutoring, Mrs. Jamison always pushed me and said to believe in myself more. The first test, I was lost, I had missed some days out of school due to my sickness and had no clue how to work those problems. When I retested, it was totally different, I was confident about passing. I passed when the results came back.

Next, I had the biology test coming up. On my first try, I failed but after being refreshed in tutorial and having a chance to retest, I passed this one just like the Algebra 1. Growing up in school, I had always been afraid to fail at anything. Every time I had homework; I would always make sure I stayed on top of things so I could be the best at what I do. When I became sick, changes took a toll on me. Surely, there have been people who've experienced what I have and have dropped out of school or committed suicide but God had better in store for me. He saw fit for me to push forward and be greater and I thank Him for that. Although, I took those tests a second time, I was delayed but I definitely was not denied. Every night I went to bed I had thoughts of not waking up the next morning, but when I did wake up the next morning to see that GOD had given me another chance to live, I was motivated to fight a little more. My mind was set on winning the battle instead of giving it up and letting it win over me. Yes! I got discouraged. Yes! I felt like I didn't want to live anymore. Yes! I wanted to throw in the towel but God was right there to lift me every time I felt like this disorder had me bound.

A Major Progress

As the time passed, I got back in the groove of going places liking shopping, out to eat, etc. This one particular Saturday, I decided I would go out with the new boy I met when I went back to school by the name of Kamian Hudson. We went bowling and out to eat. Of course, my aunt took us. I was only in the ninth grade and he was in the 10th grade. I know he thought I was crazy because I had only talked to him at school and on the phone and we had not gone out or spent any time together. I was afraid if I told him what was going on with me, he would stop talking to me. After a day of going out to eat and bowling, I came to a conclusion to tell him. He cried with me and instantly felt my pain and accepted me for who I was. At that time, he was Heaven sent from above because I had lost all of my friends when I was going through my anxiety and depression. The day I laid eyes on him at tutorial I knew then that we would click just right. We went a year strong until he had to move back home to Indianola, MS and I was not feeling that it. Although he moved back, he made sure to come and see me on the weekends. To me, it felt like every time I got happy the devil always came to destroy my happiness. Another Saturday came and I decided to attend a parade with my aunts in Greenville, MS. The only reason I went was because Kamian told me he would be there and we would meet up. When we got there, I called him to see where he was. He told me that the person he was riding with had changed their mind about coming. I instantly got upset, because I had gotten so used to him going places with me. While we waited in front of some apartments for the parade to start, I started to feel like I would faint and I needed water. The guy next to me, brought me water but the color of it was brown and it tasted like Dr. Tichenor's mouthwash. After taking a sip, I had an anxiety attack thinking that the guy tried to poison me. I did not know at the time that was the natural color of Greenville water. To calm down from my attack, my aunt walked me to the car. When I got to the car, I got my phone and called my mom but I had no idea she was attending a funeral. All I could hear was hollering and screaming in the background from broken hearts of people that had lost their loved one. I could barely hear my mom so I hung up and started to scream and cry, thinking I would be next. When I did calm down, the parade was over and we were headed to eat. My family was always a big fan of "Piccadilly" but they knew I loved Garfield's, so they gave me money to go there. Me and my youngest aunt had walked the mall hallway to see Garfield's so that I would feel better. When we got inside Garfield's and sat down, I ordered my favorite, "The Big Flav Plater." I was hungry but I just could not eat, so I asked for a carry out to take home. When I got home, I still did not have an appetite to eat at all. It was so hard for me to take anything down before I got back in the mood. All I did was drink water, chew gum and each day my weight dropped little by little. My family was afraid that I would have to be on a feeding tube if I had not eaten anything. The next day, my oldest uncle had gotten word that I was not eating so he drove to Double Quick and got me a plate of food. Upon his arrival, he informed me to eat a little bit of something every day so I could get my weight back up. When I was going through this, I never thought so many people cared about me, to see them so worried and concerned, made me so emotional. I asked GOD to please let me get back to my normal self. Major emotions came upon me when my Godfather Willie B. Pitchford came to visit me. I could see in his eyes that he was really concerned about me. After his visit with me he made sure he checked on me every day up until I got well, and I really appreciate him for that.

The Set Back

My weight went from 130 to 115, my hair came out and my skin was dry and pale. I had become weak again and my mom had to do a lot for me. One day, I decided to look in the mirror and saw that I was a totally different person. While standing there looking in the mirror, I began to cry because I knew I was not myself. Standing there, I began to talk to God and I again asked Him to heal me and bring me back to my normal self. In the midst of talking to Him, I felt as if my soul was leaving my body. I yelled for my mom and told her that I needed to get to the hospital quick. Yes! I scared her but I also was scared myself. She called my aunt to take us to the hospital. When we got there, my mom signed me in and we waited in the waiting area to be called into a room. While waiting, I asked every nurse that passed by if I was going to be ok. They were so lost because they had no idea what was going on with me until my mom explained my condition to them. When I did get called into a room, I got sick even more. The nurse Linda Mack came in to check my vitals and I was running a fever of 101.9. She had the janitor to come in to clean up after me and then she did lab work. After doing the lab work, she had a talk with me and explained that I needed to stop worrying about her nephew because he was alright. Her Nephew is my church member Justin, who was killed in a car accident, as I mentioned, in the first chapter. She mentioned to me about seeking counseling from my Pastor or

Deacons of the church, instead of constantly being put on depression medicine that was not good for my body. I took her word but I did not go to either of them about my problems because I knew it would have been all over the church and the town. The lab work came back, my Hemoglobin was high because of the medicine I was taking and it was affecting my liver. Dr. Thompson told me that my eyes should have been yellow like mustard but they were not, so she called it strange. She took me off of the medicine I was on and told me to come back next week so she could do another lab. When I went back, my lab was normal so she put me on one pill called Fluoxetine for morning nerves, but I ended up taking that pill at night because it made me sick on the stomach as well.

God Burst the Bubble

The month of February approached and that's the month we've always celebrated for grandfather's birthday. My family had already planned him a surprise party but I knew nothing about it. They were scared that I would tell him. I found out two days before the party and I was the one getting him there. With my disorder, I thought to myself, "why would they put me up to do something like this?" but I shook it off and went with the plan. I told him that I wanted him to take pictures with me. That was my way of getting him to his party. Taking pictures is something that he and I did every year to advertise our grandfather and grand-daughter bond. The day of the party, we both dressed up in red and black. He never picked his own clothes Lol! My aunt and I always dressed him. We dressed in those colors because they were the colors of the decorations for his party. He picked me up from home and we headed to this church where we took the pictures at every year, but of course, when we got there no one was taking pictures. We got back in the truck and I told him that we should check the Hooper Center to see if they were taking them there. That was the place his surprise party was being held. Before we proceeded there, I told him that I was hungry and I wanted to go to Subway. Yes! My aunt texted me and told me they were not ready for him yet. I was nervous as if they were surprising me. By the time my sandwich was fixed, my aunt had texted again and said they were all set and ready for my grandfather. When we pulled up to the building, he noticed a lot of cars were there and he told me if the line was too long, we could come back and take the pictures. We walked up to the building and as we walked in, my family yelled SURPRISE! The joy that I had seeing my distant and close family together, had me feeling like that party was for me. He looked at me and said, "There is nobody in here set up to take no pictures" we hugged and laughed a while about how we surprised him. Being at the party around my family, I started to feel like myself again. I felt FREE, I had joy, laughter, and I felt like I did before I developed the disorder. Then, my aunt got sick in the midst of all the joy. She started to vomit in the garbage can and fainted right after. Everyone ran to help her and I ran out of the door crying and having an anxiety attack. With me being so happy and back to myself, I just could not take what was going on around me. I felt as if the devil was trying to attack my family for no reason; including me. My aunt was rushed to the hospital in Belzoni, MS., where they told her that she had the flu and was dehydrated. After she was released from the hospital, we all gathered at my grandfather's house and my heart was still filled with emotions but my anxiety had stopped. The next day was Sunday and it was time for my family to go back home. I was not ready for all that. That morning, I began to cry and my late cousin Kathy Grace Smith questioned me about why was I crying? I told her I did not know. She asked me was it because they were leaving and I again I said no because I did not want them to worry about me. When everybody packed up and said their goodbyes, I began to feel like I was in a bubble again. The joy had left that quick from Saturday to Sunday. I was not happy anymore, I did not have any joy, I had not one laugh left in me. That same night, I got on my knees again and I asked God again if He did not do anything else for me, I just wanted Him to heal me. The next week my cousin Pastor Charles Edwards Sr., came over to pray for me and he had me repeat these scriptures after him; Psalms 23:4 "Yea, though I walk through the valley of the shadows of death, I will fear no evil. For thou art with me, thy rod and thy staff, they comfort me. 5. Thou preparest a table before me in the presence of mine enemies: thou anointest my head with oil; my cup runneth over. 6. Surely goodness and mercy shall follow me all the days of my life: and I will dwell in the house of the LORD forever." **(Psalms 23:4-6 KJV)**

He prayed for me and told me to keep the faith and to trust God. I did what he told me to do and I could remember Elder Watson asking God to rebuke everything that had me bound. I began to ask God the same thing in my prayers and I was better in no time. A lot of people question God but my question to them is, HOW COULD YOU QUESTION HIM? I never questioned God, why this was happening to me. I just prayed and asked Him to heal me, he did just that. I asked Him to set me free and I was set free just when I was about to give up. We all have heard of the saying, "He may not come when you want Him too, but He's always on time." That saying is so true because God was right on time when I was just about to give up and throw in the towel. He made me try Him, up until the very last strength I had. It took 3 months for me to get back to reality but guess what? I'm still here, I'm alive, God healed me right on time, and He has not left me since. I am a living testimony. There were so many times that I wanted to get up and tell my testimony at church but I just could not find the gut to get up and speak. No! I was not ashamed of what GOD had done for me. No! I was not scared. No! My mind was not always blank. Deep down inside GOD was telling me to share this story elsewhere but I did not have a clue where He was telling me to tell my story. I started to share it with people one on one. I got the confidence to share some of it on Facebook but I still was not sure how well my story had gotten out there. Three years ago, God put it on my heart to write a book but I did not know where to start. This wonderful lady of God Andrea Allen of Belzoni, MS., had just gotten her book published and it gave me the inspiration to write one. I started writing once but I lost hope. This year, 2019, my former teacher Erica Boyd of Indianola, MS., wrote a book and got hers published. I then told myself that I could do anything if I just put my mind to it. Now here I am, sitting here writing my own book. Won't He do it?

Pre-Prepared

To make a long story so understanding, GOD was preparing me for something that He knew would take place in my life 2-5 years later. He was exposing me to depression, anxiety, and grief while I had all of my loved ones on earth and close to me. With me already being exposed, He knew that depression, grief, and anxiety would not kill me. God knew how much I could bare at the time I was going through my condition, and lost my loved one's years later. He had already prepared me for what He knew would be the worst time of my life. Being that He knows all things, He broke those time periods. He called a close friend home first to get me prepared for my close loved ones. If I had not been exposed to depression, grief, and anxiety, it would have taken me out at once but He knows best in all situations. He saw fit to have better plans for me. He did not let me give in. When I lost my loved ones I cried, screamed, I was lonely, I needed a hug, sleepless nights and I did not know what to do; but guess what? I was not depressed, I was not in deep grief, and I did not have any anxiety attacks because I was already prepared. February 14, 2014, I went to school like a normal day, ready to receive a gift from my Valentine and pig out at the Valentine Party we had planned at vocational. I had so much joy that day. I ate so much food that I could barely walk. When school was out, my mom picked me up. The entire time she was on the phone talking to someone but she was really talking in code so I could not understand what she was really talking about. As she began to mention hospital and life support, I began to question her. Yes! I was being disrespectful while she was on the phone because I knew then that something was not right. She finally told me that my favorite cousin, that's more like a sister to me, Kathy Grace Smith was in the hospital on life support and the doctors told my aunt that she would not make it through the night. I could not believe what I was hearing, so I asked her to repeat it again. When she repeated what she had told me, I tried to pray but I just could not find the words to pray so I started to cry. When we arrived at my Grandfather's house, my Grandmother began to call all the family to let them know. While she did that, I began to get chills all over my body. I could not take what was going on at the moment. Thoughts started going through my head about me being left in this cold world without her. We were like two peas in a pot, until she had to move away to Memphis, TN. When you saw her, you saw me! We were more like sisters than cousins because that's how our parents raised us to stick together. That night around 8 p.m., it was confirmed that she was deceased. For a minute, I completely lost it until my mom reminded me about how I did not want to be bound in depression, grief, or anxiety again. So every day, I asked GOD to give me strength and be with my family and I. Everybody was crazy at this time because it had been 19 years since we had lost an immediate family member, which was my late

Great Grandmother Viola Body to breast cancer. She was the wife of my main man, mentioned in the first couple chapters, the late Hugh "Junior" Body. I never got to meet her. She passed away 3 years before I was born but from what I heard; she was one of a kind. Death is something that no one gets used to but it's something that we all have to deal with someday. Friday came and it was the weekend to bury my ride or die, my sister, my best friend Kathy Grace Smith. As the time passed on the clock, I was not ready but I knew I had to go and be with my family in the time of sorrow. When I saw her in the coffin, my heart began to fill with pain because there was nothing I could do. I had plenty of emotions but GOD allowed me to control myself because He knew I did not want to be back at square one. That night we had a get together at the community building in town called the Facility Building. I felt better when I got there because I had the opportunity to see all of my family but every second, I realized that I was missing my best friend. The next day came and it was time to lay her to rest. The funeral was held at the High School Auditorium, the same place my church members' funeral was held. Everybody got up that morning getting ready, but also dreading the day that we would have to leave Kathy Grace in a grave and never see her again. During the funeral, I looked around to see if any of my friends or classmates were there but I didn't see a soul. The only person that showed up and stuck by my side was my cousin, Kimberly Roscoe and I really appreciated her for that.

When Kathy attended Humphreys County High School, she was the class of 2013 and they all came and showed a lot of love and support. When the funeral was over, it was time for the burial and I was not ready at all. As I watched the vault staff roll her down, I began to feel the knots in my stomach. When we made it to the repast, I could not eat anything. At that moment, I did not understand at all but there was no way I would question GOD. I wanted it all to be a dream, but this was really reality. She lost her life at 19-years-old. She did not get a chance to even live her life. No kids, no husband, and she had only accomplished part of her dream by starting hair school. She was her mother's only child and that made her death sadden people more and more.

Understanding Death

After the funeral and the days passed, I tried to think about everything on the brighter side but I could not because we had no closure as a family. When Kathy Grace came to Mississippi two weeks before, she told us she was anemic and complained that her stomach was hurting but I had no idea she was dying. Her face was all broke out but I thought it was from some makeup or a lotion she had used. She was weak but I thought it was from her stomach pain. I began to think about it in a way that I could move on from. I thought to myself, if she had lived with whatever she had then she would have to suffer and she would be in pain and I knew I didn't want her to suffer so I asked GOD to help me accept the fact that she was gone. Earlier in that month, February 5, 2014, my Great Grandmother Mrs. Ethel Bullock had passed away as well. I watched her suffer for four days from breast cancer, after being put on life support. She would sit up but she could not talk or focus her eyes on me. This one particular day, I went in to see her with my aunt Vivian and she had her eyes toward my direction, the only thing I could do was stare because I could not believe this was actually happening to her. My aunt Vivian looked at me and said, "talk to her baby, she wants you to say something to her" but I could not find the right words to say. That was my first time ever seeing someone on life support and I did not know it could drain a person who was in good health. After she was buried, I got a text from my late cousin Kathy and she told me she was sorry for my loss and asked was I ok. I told her I was fine, but little did I know, she would be the next person to go. As time passed, I had gotten better at dealing with death until I lost the love of my life.

A Major Decline

The same year my cousin passed away, my grandfather had to have a defibrillator implanted in his chest due to congestive heart failure. After having it implanted, he continued to do good until two years later. His health took a toll. He went from going to church every Sunday, to not being able to make it to church at all. For two years, he had several doctor's appointments and procedures to make sure he was in good health. First, he started off using a crutch in 2016. Then, he started using a walker in 2017 and months into that year he was wheelchair bound. Congestive Heart Failure had gotten the best of him. In other people's eyes he was sick, but in my eyes, he was still the same. When I realized he was declining, I signed up for the Certified Nursing Assistant program at Mississippi Delta Community College to learn how to take better care of him. The year of 2016, he had been in and out of the hospital due to his blood pressure being so low. We had gotten used to it as a family because he always returned back home better than before. The year of 2017, I started and completed the certified nursing assistant program and that was the best path I had ever taken because he needed me more than anything. I went to school in the morning and I took care of him in the evening. The skills I had learned, prepared me to meet everything he needed. Bathing, feeding, position in a wheelchair, peri care and more. He was so proud that I had taken that route just to take care of him but I had no idea that he would not bounce back. My main man was a brick mason and he was built ford tough in my eyes. I never saw him down before the illness. He had to check his weight, blood pressure, and heart rate on a daily basis. This one particular day, I came home from school and his blood pressure was running 84/24 and at that moment I knew something was not right. He had a nurse that came in the morning to check it but when I got out of school, I always checked it again. I notified my mom and aunt so we could get him to the hospital. My aunt arrived and we drove him to the Indianola hospital. They told us that he needed to be hospitalized, so his blood pressure could regulate. I was also working in Greenwood at the time on second shift from 3pm until 11pm. I worked rotation days, 4 on and 2 days off while going to school in the morning time. On my last day off, I would take extra clothes to work and after work, I went to the hospital to stay with him on my two days off. I did that until he was released from the hospital. One week, when I went back to work, he ended up falling and it left him with a big gash on his head. When I questioned him about it, he said that the nurse hit him, but when others asked him, he said he thought he could walk again and ended up falling. We could not blame anyone because he was telling two different stories. When he got released from the hospital my cousin Bernard and I were there to pick him up. He said to me "If you don't do nothing else for me please take me home away from this place." I got him out of that place and proceeded to take him home but we could not seem to make it to our destination, because he was vomiting all over my car. I pulled over twice to tend to him, and then we finally made it home. As soon as we got to the house, I checked his vitals and his blood pressure was lower than it had ever been before. We as a family came to an agreement to call an ambulance and have him taken elsewhere for a second opinion. They took him to Greenwood Leflore Hospital. I was satisfied because that was more convenient for me being that was the town, I worked in. Of course, he was admitted to that hospital and after tests had been ran, it was confirmed that he had a heart attack hours before arriving to the hospital. Every day on my 15-minute break I used my time to see him. There were nights, I skipped eating just to get that time I needed with him to make sure he was ok. On weekends, we all met as a family to visit him upon the ICU hours. When his three weeks was up there, he got transferred to the Select Specialty Hospital in Greenville, MS. I was so disappointed because that was totally out of the way of the route I had to take to my job. It was so hard getting back and forth over there to see him when I was a full-time student and I worked a full-time job, but I managed to see him twice a week. On my days off, I wanted to spend the night with him but this place was totally different from normal hospitals. They didn't want anyone to spend the night and when we asked, they never gave us a place to lay our heads. They only had two hard Geri chairs for visitors, and there was no way anyone would be comfortable sleeping in those. When I did go to visit him, I stayed 4 hours or more unless I had to go to work. Since I was certified as a Nursing Assistant, the CNA's didn't have to come by his room because I did all of his personal care; from feeding to bathing. Being that I worked in a facility, I knew exactly how things went from not bathing a patient to leaving a patient soaking wet, and that's why I was so strict about him. I would pop up any time of the day when I was off work, just to make sure he was being treated properly. I never treated anyone's family different when I worked because I didn't want anyone treating him or any of my family members badly. During his hospital stay, my uncle lost his ex-wife which was still a daughter-in-law to my grandfather. We had her funeral, buried her and all, and he didn't know a thing about it. I felt so guilty because I had never hidden a family matter like that from my grandfather. I was always the one he depended on to tell him if anything was going wrong. The week after the funeral was over, I talked it over with my uncle about telling him about her death. He told me that I should go ahead and tell him before someone else told him. I asked my cousin Bernard to ride with me to break the news to my grandfather because I could not do it alone. When we told him, he replied, "I thought she had gotten better?" I said, "she did but she passed out and didn't come back through." He was silent the entire time as if he was in shock for 20 minutes and he soon started to engage back in conversation with us. I assured him that everything was taken care of and my uncle; his son, didn't have to go through anything alone. I felt so guilty because the funeral had already passed and I was just telling him what had happened. Before I left the hospital, the nurse notified me that he hadn't had a bowel movement and all he was doing was sleeping and urinating. She was giving me a hint of what was about to happen, but I didn't worry too much because some older people have bowel complications when their diet changes. Driving back home, I felt guilty once again because I had kept that from him, I began to get emotional about both situations with my aunt passing away and my grandfather being in the hospital and not doing so well. Instead of them giving condolences about my aunt, they had mistaken her passing for my grandfather. I was so hurt because they were killing him before his time was up.

I Died Mentally, He Died Spiritually

The next week on a Wednesday, I didn't have class that morning so I made it my business to go see my grandfather before work, when I got there it was lunch time. I noticed the food was pureed, but I still encouraged him to eat because he was basically living off of Ensure and Water. He wouldn't pick up the spoon and eat himself, so I started to feed him. It hurt my feelings because I thought I was going as slow as possible while feeding him. Minutes later, I realized he just didn't want the food at all. I talked it over with his nurse and she assured me that I could go get him some Kentucky Fried Chicken because that was all he would eat. I went out and got some chicken but by the time I came back, it was time for me to be back at work. I fed him for 5 minutes then I let his nurse take over. I told him 10 times, that I was about to go, until the point where he got mad and said, "go head if you're going" that hurt my feelings because he had never been so mean to me. I went on to work and I didn't think anything more about it until his nurse called me that night and told me he didn't want any more of the food after I left. The next day was Thursday, while heading to school I realized I had left my Bluetooth headphones in his room at the hospital, while waiting outside for class to start I called the hospital to see if anyone had seen my headphones but no one had seen them. After talking to the nurse, I asked if I could speak to my grandfather. I cannot remember the entire conversation but he was in good spirits, he asked about the weather, how school was going, and about everyone back at the house. I told him that the weather was good and everything and everybody was doing just fine and that I would see him Saturday which was my next day off. The day after that was Friday, I went to work like a normal day. When it was time to go on break it was so cold outside to the point where I could barely stand it and my co-worker/friend Kelsey Scott, RN let me borrow her coat to go out and get something to eat. When I came back, I saw two of my other co-workers standing outside chatting so I joined them for a couple of minutes and while talking to them my eyes began to focus on the sky and I saw a falling star. They say when you see one falling you should make a wish, so I wished my Grandfather would be healed. When the night of work was over, I explained to my co-worker which is my best friend Audriel. I shared with her that I could not stand the cool front that came around break time. I dropped her off in Indianola, MS. and I headed home alone. When I arrived at home, I walked in the door and before I could close it my mom yelled down stairs and told me that we needed to head over to Greenville hospital because my grandfather had gotten worse and my heart dropped instantly! I waited around on everyone to get ready because I could not drive myself at that moment. I was stuck! My aunt Toya drove me in my car and my mom and other's rode with my aunt Rosie. It took us so long to get there, I thought the worst the entire ride there but I didn't know that the outcome would be death. When we pulled up to the parking lot my uncle Chris was standing outside by his car. We got out and noticed he had water running down his face, he normally deals with allergies so I had to ask was he crying? and the reason why he was crying? He replied "DAD DIED" I asked no further questions I ran in the hospital thinking I could save him but GOD had already called him home an hour before we arrived at the hospital. When I ran in the hospital, I saw my mom, my aunt Debra, and uncle Terry sitting there crying their hearts out. I could not believe it so I asked my mom again was it true? When she said yes! I instantly lost my mind at that moment, hollering, crying, and falling all out on the floor. They told me in order for me to see my grandfather I had to get myself together first, I got myself together because I really wanted to see him. When I did go back to see him, I started hollering, crying, and falling out again. They took me back out to the waiting room but when I was calm again, I asked to go back in there because I could not believe what I was hearing or seeing. As I felt my stomach getting weak, I went to the waiting room again but this time I did not go back to the room where my grandfather was. After the Martians picked him up, we all walked out of the hospital as one big family with majorly broken hearts. October 28, 2017 GOD healed him spiritually and I died mentally. I wanted to give up on school, friendships, my relationship, my job, and even my life, but I came to the realization that it was his time not mines and GOD still had a purpose for me on this earth. When we got home from the hospital it was around three or four in the morning so everyone went home to rest and we met back up at my grandfather's house the next day. When I woke up that morning, I went to my mom's room and I asked her was it true that my grandfather had died or was I dreaming. When she told me, it was true I started hollering and crying again. I wondered why this was happening but I never questioned GOD. The rest of the weekend I was surrounded with my family but a part of me was missing. I accepted condolences but deep inside I wanted to die. The devil was riding us bad and I think his plan was to take me out like before, but GOD had a plan for it all. He gave me and my family strength and guidance during the time of sorrow. The next week was even harder for me because we had to make arrangements, get ourselves together, and prepare to lay my grandfather to rest on Saturday. The entire week my moods were up and down. Friday came and it was time to see him in a coffin. I was the first one to see him. As I walked into the funeral home, I felt my body getting weak but I continuously asked GOD for strength. Walking into the visitation room I could see him lying there from afar but I could not recognize him, as I got closer and closer, he began to look more like himself. When I got close, I began to cry, I placed his red man tobacco in his coat pocket along with a pack of double mint gum. Those were the two things he always kept on him and I made sure he had them. While putting the gum and tobacco in my grandfather's pocket, I felt someone behind me rubbing my back, it was Pyron Smith the same woman of GOD who helped her mom pray for me doing my depression stage as I mentioned in the previous chapters. She told me to let it out and take as much time as I needed to. Ms. Pyron got me a chair and I sat right in front of the coffin, not believing what I was seeing. As I got up to try to hug him in the casket I was so broken to the point where I just begun to shake. When I calmed down, I sat there talking to him just as he was still alive until the rest of the family arrived. Just to see my mom, grandma, and the rest of my family cry, broke me down again. All I remember was someone carrying me out of the funeral home. That was the worst pain I had ever felt but I didn't give in because I knew that GOD was still able. The night after the visitation we had a family get together at the Hooper center. Everything was going good until my aunt didn't want my uncle from Chicago, IL saying anything to her and all hell broke loose. I knew then it was time for me to go. By that time the shirts for the family were ready to be picked up, but when I got them, I said to myself I am not giving out shirts until they learn how to act. The next day it was time to lay my grandfather to rest but we ran into a problem. The road to the cemetery was too muddy for the funeral cars to drive on. We needed a plan B and my uncle Marcus and his friends thought of a quick plan.

The plan was to get two trailers and two four wheelers to bury him. Before his homegoing service they got everything ready so we wouldn't have to worry about anything. He was the first to be buried that way but if it wasn't for the mud, they wouldn't have ever thought of such a thing. He grew up as a country boy so everything blended right together. The funeral was held at the High School Auditorium at 1:00pm. As time passed, my stomach got weaker by the hour. I could not believe I was about to say goodbye to the love of my life forever. Walking down the aisle to view him I felt my body getting lighter. I began to pray to GOD for strength because I didn't want to pass out and miss his homegoing. While the service was going on, I was so out of my body to the point where I barely remembered who was sitting in the audience as visitors. I became alert when my uncle had to be taken out in the middle of the service, being that I was in the health field I had to make sure he was okay. My grandfather had a nice but sad home going. The service was packed but not like I expected it to be. I cried a couple of times but I praised GOD in spite of, because I had done my part and I knew He would carry my family and I through, despite what it looked like. After the funeral we proceeded to the burial. The family cars parked us on the church parking lot and we all loaded one trailer with him in the middle of us and the rest of the family loaded the other trailer. Some brought boots and some had bags on their feet. The ride to the gravesite was breathtaking to me and the weather was just right. While riding, the sun shined down on me and I could hear my grandfather telling me that everything would be okay. It was so hard to see the one who raised and nurtured me to the woman I was that day, being rolled down into a lonely grave that I would never see again until GOD calls me home. At the repast I didn't have an appetite but I tried to eat anyway until my plate looked played over. As I mingled with my family, some I see every day, some I hadn't seen in years, it crossed my mind again that he was missing. Back at the house that night my uncle's friends cooked fish and BBQ for the family. I just could not believe we were having a party after my grandfather had been put to rest. Life says you have to go on but, in my mind, I was still stuck at the hospital that night wondering what went wrong. While everybody was mingling, I was trying to get myself together until I saw my uncle knock a guy out cold. I thought instantly it was one of our family members but when I got closer it was just an old drunk off the street talking mess that we didn't want to hear. The next day came and it was time for everyone to go back home. My heart was crushed because the only thing that was keeping me going was their love. It was not easy at all the first couple of weeks. We all cried and grieved. GOD allowed me to be strong enough to encourage my little brother that we could make it through that time of sorrow. He was only eight years old when my grandfather departed from this world. They had a bond as if they were father and son instead of great-grandfather and great-grandson. Being that he was so young and they were so close, he had no understanding at all. He just wanted to know why our grandfather had to go. The enemy thought he would overtake my family after that loss but GOD proved him wrong. Even though we were broken to pieces we still asked GOD for strength daily. The devil thought he would bind me again with depression and grief but GOD already had me prepared from the first time I went through it. I had always said if I ever lost my grandfather that I would probably lose my mind because he was my back bone, but here I am now writing a book and doing just fine 2 and a half years later. "Somebody ought to praise him!" Of course, I have my days but the emotions only come for a moment and I'm back to myself a day or minutes later. As you read through my story you can see that I have had some hard times in life but I'm still here because GOD has a purpose for my life. Oftentimes I am told that He wants to use me to help other people and now I have become a firm believer of that. My story cannot only help someone going through depression, grief, or anxiety, but can heal someone that's going through a totally different situation such as cancer, just by reading about the way GOD healed me. I never got up in church and told my testimony, this was one of the testimonies I have sat down on for years, because I knew I wouldn't be able to tell the entire story. I thought if I wrote a book, I could tell every detail and bless others tremendously. One thing about me, as I have already mentioned above, I'll never be ashamed to share with others about the things that GOD has done for me. I just want to encourage somebody to try him! Trust him! And Believe in him!

Life without Him

A week had passed since my grandfather had been gone and it finally hit in my heart that I'll never be able to hear his voice again or do anything for him anymore. I felt like an animal who had wandered off from its mother and could not find its way back home. My heart felt like it lived in a deep freezer. Everywhere I went and everything I saw made me think of him. To me, my family was like a kingdom who had lost their KING. Nobody could seem to focus without him. He had always been like a king to us. He would lead, and we would follow. He carried all of us. He took care of all of us. He prayed for all of us. He paid for all of our tithes. He fed all of us. He nurtured all of us. He put all of us through school. We were all his kids. When he left this world, everybody seemed grumpy and over taken by the devil. There were times that disagreements turned into arguments, and I was the one to always remind them that he raised us so much better than that. With him being gone, life was not the same at all and it still isn't. The things he used to get us through and the things he used to do for us, he could no longer do anymore. He left us like a toddler that was put out into the world to take care of himself alone. That's how rotten and crippled he had us. There was nothing that any of us asked for that we did not get. He took care of his children, grandchildren, and great-grands the same. Anytime I was sick I didn't want him out of my sight and I began to wonder what if I encountered a major sickness without him being here on this earth, how would I get through it on my own. It brought me back to my condition that was mentioned in the previous chapters. Nobody was able to help me through it but GOD, and if I was to encounter such in the future, GOD will do the same thing for me as He did before, because He is the same GOD. See, He takes us through things we don't understand to show us how to trust Him. That's exactly what He did for my family. Many people wondered how we made it through all of the grief, struggles, pain, and heartaches being that my grandfather was our backbone. Let me tell you what we did; we were trusting and believing in Him and that's how we made it over. There were times when He didn't show up at the moment, we needed Him, but we knew He was still able. All those nights we cried ourselves to sleep we never lost our trust in the Lord and that's how we made it. He never left the BODY FAMILY alone and I'm truly grateful and thankful for that. A year later I decided to contact the Mississippi Department of Transportation to adopt a highway in memory of my grandfather. I chose highway 12 in Belzoni, MS. That's where he was born and raised. Our family church sits right off that highway by the name of Day Break M.B. church. Now as you approach the highway a mile in between both ends you will see a sign that says "In Loving Memory of HUGH JUNIOR BODY." As a family we made an agreement to the Mississippi Department of transportation that we would clean up between the two signs twice every season to keep the sign in place. Every season my family and I have been doing just that. Every time I travel the highway the sign catches my eye sitting so stunning, and it motivates me each time "to stick with it." Those are the words my grandfather would tell people if he saw them trying to have something in life.

The Church Termination Letter

The grief was just beginning to ease, the heartaches had finally stopped and I was getting back to myself after encountering the major loss of my grandfather. January 2019, I had just decided that I would start to go to church every third Sunday and pay my 10 percent of the tithes. God had also put it on my mind to start sowing seeds. The Sunday before I got ready to start this journey, I received a letter in the mail on January 21, 2019 along with five more of my family members notifying us that we had been terminated from our generation church based on prescribed criteria within the by-laws of the church. My other family members didn't seem to be bothered but I was totally pressed. I was told to contact the moderator of Belzoni, MS. We spoke and he told me that the church had the right to send letters out if we had been issued by-laws and had not followed through with them. I told him that I have always been a smart and nosey girl and I had never witnessed the church issuing any by-laws and I asked around and no one could seem to show me any by-laws. He told me that he would call a meeting with the deacons to see if they could get to the bottom of the situation of why they were terminating members and had not given out any by-laws. I could not believe it at all. The church I grew up in, got baptized at, and accepted Christ at the age of 10. The church I sung in the junior choir at, said Easter speeches, performed in Christmas plays and praise danced at. I was hurt! I could not believe I was being taken off the church roll for missing a certain number of Sundays and a few months behind on my tithes. We only had service on third Sunday's and as I mentioned in the chapter before this one, my grandfather always paid my tithes. He was the head deacon of the church. When he went home to be with the Lord the last thing on my mind was keeping up with my tithes and paying church salary. I was just beginning to be a woman and learning how to take care of myself. The letter had me so upset to the point where I posted it on Facebook for others opinion. Most went against it like I did and a few was all for it. I got into an argument with a couple of the church members but they didn't know how I felt. They were not in my shoes. On another note, they wonder why people don't attend church on a regular, because of judgmental people and uncalled for situations like this. After receiving the letter, I went through depression again, but no one knew it because it was a mild stage and I knew exactly how to control it. My heart was shattered because I knew the only one who could give me the best advice was my grandfather, and he couldn't tell me a thing. That's when I was reminded about the man up above, who he always taught me to lean and depend on. I began to ask GOD for directions. I was lost. I didn't know what to do. My mind was telling me to find another church home but my heart was telling me to rejoin the same exact church. While waiting for GOD to give me directions I visited Shiloh Deovelente M.B. Church where my cousin Charles Edwards Sr. is the pastor. While sitting in the service I felt welcomed, the choir was singing just right, and the message he brought that Sunday was just for me. When it was time for altar prayer, he begins to sing the song "When I see Jesus." Tears began to roll down my face and I started to think about my grandfather and what direction he would want me to go. I went to the altar and Pastor Edwards prayed for GOD to give me direction. While he was praying for me I could feel GOD telling me that was the church I needed to be a part of but my mind was telling me that I needed to return to Daybreak and make it right with them. My thoughts were going back and forth like two people battling against one another to win a fight. After service, I had several members encouraging me to become a part of the church family but the enemy was still playing with my mind. There was no way I could go back to Daybreak after the burden they had brought upon me. I knew I wouldn't be comfortable at all. At this moment I still do not have a church home but I often visit Shiloh and pay my tithes at New Life St. Paul where I learned how to become healed and set free. Before this book is finished my plan is to join Shiloh Deovelente and become a faithful member. Everything happens for a reason, so maybe the letter was a sign from GOD telling me to move on despite of the church being generational. I would often have thoughts of my grandfather flipping over in his grave, if I moved my membership to another church before I had gotten the letter. Now that I have received the letter, I often wonder what his thoughts and inputs would have been. Nevertheless, I pray that he helps me make the right decision and be happy with whatever decision I make. Some people may look at it as not being a big deal, but to me it is because I had never been the type to be out of church for a long period of time. I was raised in church and without having a church home, it feels so different. I never once imagined something like this happening to me.

The Greatness of God

If I had a million tongues, I still couldn't thank GOD enough for bringing me out. He didn't have to do it but He did. He thought I was worth saving. He had better plans and a purpose for my life. He was better to me than I was to myself. There were times that I forgot to pray but He still blessed me anyway. Millions didn't make it, but I was one of the ones who did, and I'll forever thank Him for that. He has been so good to me! He has never left me alone. There are times that I sit and think about all of the things He has done for me and the rest of His children. Then I think about where we'll be without Him. Sometimes I take my pen and write down in my notebook the numerous things He has done for me, until I can't write anymore. There's something about the name of Jesus. He can make a way out of no way. He's intentional. He's mighty. He's faithful. Most of all He's bigger than whatever problems you are facing. He's always there to carry you through despite the circumstances. I can't speak for anyone else but I can truly say that I owe Him all the praise, honor, and glory. I often encourage people to try Him, trust Him, and believe in Him. GOD can turn things around in the blink of an eye. He can work miracles. He can break the chains. He can heal you. He can deliver you. He can forgive you. He can protect you. He can guide you. He can do ALL THE ABOVE if you just open your mouth and seek Him. I've seen Him do it. I am a witness. I am a walking miracle. I am blessed.

Healed! Delivered and Set Free

Six years later GOD is still good to me and He has yet to fail me. I am healthy, strong, and most of all I have a relationship with GOD. I am 22 years of age. I received my high school diploma from Humphrey County High School. After high school I attended Mississippi Delta Community College where I received a certification as a Health Care Assistant and an associate's degree in Pre-Nursing. Later, I decided to further my education in the health field and I attended the Med Tech Training and Tutoring Program where I met the requirements and received a certificate to become a phlebotomist. I am currently a Certified Nursing assistant and employed at Martha Coker Green Houses in Yazoo City, Mississippi. As I await to be accepted into the nursing program to become a Licensed Practical Nurse, I enjoy my family, friends, patients, and everyday life. I have my own car and I'm currently in search of my own house. Whatever the devil had planned for me, it did not work. GOD HAD BETTER PLANS FOR MY LIFE. There's a saying that says what don't kill you will make you stronger, depression didn't kill me, anxiety didn't kill me, grief didn't kill me, GOD me stronger than I ever had been before and most of all He prepared me for whatever obstacle that was coming up next in my life. Everything I was going through was way too big for me. There was no way I could get through it on my own. Thank you, GOD! I am a survivor, I am a true blessing, and last but not least I am living witness that prayer does change things. I am healed, delivered and SET FREE!

Made in the USA
Columbia, SC
12 February 2024